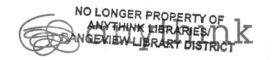

D1475430

ICE CREAM

Kitchen Experiment

By Meg Gaertner

Published by The Child's World®
1980 Lookout Drive • Mankato, MN 56003-1705
800-599-READ • www.childsworld.com

Photographs ©: Rick Orndorf, cover, 1, 14, 16, 17, 18, 19, 20, 21; Africa
Studio/Shutterstock Images, 5; iStockphoto, 6, 13; Tom Wang/Shutterstock
Images, 7; Shutterstock Images, 9; Steve Debenport/iStockphoto, 10

ISBN 9781503825390
LCCN 2017959693

Printed in the United States of America
PA02378

Table of Contents

CHAPTER 1

Hot and Cold

We say things are hot or cold all the time. But what does this mean? Heat has to do with how fast **atoms** move. Everything is made of atoms.

Atoms move around inside of things. **Temperature** tells us how fast atoms move around. At high temperatures, atoms move around a lot. They bump into each other. Something that has a high temperature is hot. Hot chocolate is hot. At low temperatures, atoms slow down. They stay closer together.

Hot chocolate is a hot drink. It can be served with marshmallows.

Something that has a low temperature is cold. Ice cream is cold.

Water that is very cold **freezes** into ice. Ice is a **solid**. The temperature at which this happens is called its freezing point.

Snow is ice that falls from clouds. We can go sledding on snow.

TIP
Water mixed with salt has a different freezing point. It will not freeze until it gets even colder than 32°F (0°C).

Water freezes at 32°F (0°C). This is its freezing point. When water has a higher temperature, it is a **liquid**.

Heat moves from the warm air to a cold ice pop. This is why it melts.

Heat can move from one thing to another. Heat always moves from hot things to cold things. This is why a cold drink gets warmer. Heat moves from the warm air to the cold drink. This is also why a hot drink will slowly cool. Heat moves from the warm drink to the cold air.

CHAPTER 2

Salt Does the Trick

People put salt on icy roads in the winter. They do this to melt the ice. It keeps water from freezing. Salt lowers the freezing point of water. Salt water has to get even colder before it freezes.

Ice has a thin coat of water on the outside. The salt mixes with this water. Heat moves from the warmer salt water to the ice. The ice melts. The salt water gets very cold but does not freeze. This happens because of **molecules**.

Snowplows remove snow from the road. They also spray salt to melt the ice.

Molecules are too small to see. But we can build models to look at their shapes.

Atoms come together to make molecules. These molecules form everything around us. Table salt is made from two kinds of atoms. They are sodium and chlorine. These atoms come together to form molecules of salt. When you pour salt in water, the salt molecules spread through the water.

Water freezes when its molecules are arranged in a certain way. Salt molecules get in the way. They prevent the water from freezing. The water gets colder, but it does not become ice yet.

TIP
Anything that dissolves in water lowers the freezing point of water. Salt dissolves in water. Its molecules spread out. Salt molecules mix with the water molecules.

You can use this trick to make ice cream!
Put a plastic zip bag of milk and sugar inside
a larger plastic zip bag of salt and ice. The salt
melts the ice. It makes very cold water.
The water is much colder than the milk
and sugar. Heat flows from the milk
and sugar to the water. The milk
and sugar get cold very quickly.
They freeze and make ice cream!

TIP

Some people cannot drink dairy milk. It makes them sick. You can make ice cream at home with any type of milk, such as soy milk or almond milk.

Ice cream is a tasty treat on a hot day.

CHAPTER 3

THE EXPERIMENT
Let's Make Ice Cream!

TIME TO FINISH: 15-20 minutes

15

20

MATERIALS LIST

1 cup (236 mL) milk
1/4 cup (59 mL) sugar
1/4 teaspoon (1 mL) vanilla
2 quart-size (.95 L) plastic zip bags
1 gallon-size (3.79 L) plastic zip bag
ice
1/2-3/4 cup (118-177 mL) rock salt
dishcloth
bowl
spoon

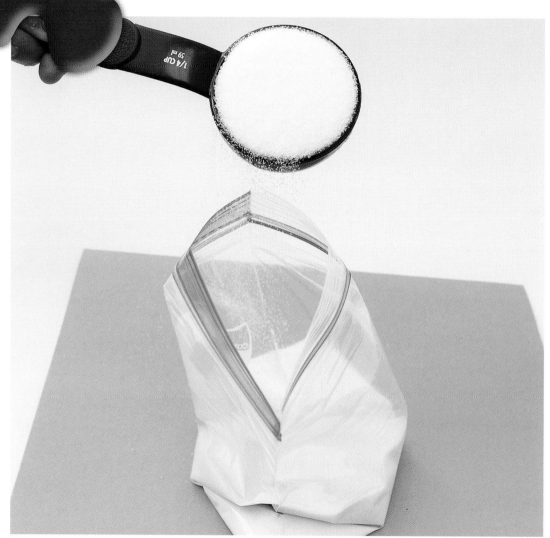

1. Add the milk, sugar, and vanilla to a small bag. Push out the extra air. Close the bag tightly.

2. Put that bag inside the second small bag. This will keep your ice cream from leaking.

3. Put ice in the bigger bag. The ice should fill half of the bag.

4. Add salt to the bag of ice.

5. Put the smaller bag in the bigger bag. Close the bigger bag.

6. Cover the bag with the dishcloth. Hold the bag and shake it from side to side.

7. Shake the bag for about 10–15 minutes. You will see the milk and sugar slowly get thicker. Keep shaking the bag until the ice cream is thick.

TIP
The bag will become cold enough to hurt your skin. The cloth will keep your hands safe.

8. Open the bigger bag. Take out the smaller bag.

9. Open the small bag.

TIP
You can check on your ice cream every few minutes. Is the ice cream not getting thick? You can add more salt to the ice if needed.

10. Scoop your ice cream into a bowl. Enjoy!

TIP
What toppings do you like on your ice cream? Sprinkles? Chocolate syrup? Nuts? You can add all kinds of fun things to your ice cream once it is ready to eat.

Glossary

atoms (AT-uhms) Atoms are the tiny bits that make up everything. Atoms are too small to see without special machines.

dissolves (di-ZOLVZ) Something dissolves in water when its molecules mix with the water molecules. Salt dissolves in water.

freezes (FREE-zez) A liquid freezes when it becomes solid at cold temperatures. Water freezes into ice.

liquid (LIK-wid) A liquid is a type of matter that can fill a container. Water is a liquid above 32°F (0°C).

molecules (MOL-uh-kyools) Molecules are groups of atoms. Salt molecules lower the freezing point of water.

solid (SOL-id) A solid is a type of matter that does not change its shape. Ice is a solid.

temperature (TEM-pur-uh-chur) Temperature is a measure of how fast atoms move around. Hot things have a high temperature.

To Learn More

In the Library

Hagler, Gina. *Step-by-Step Experiments with Matter*. Mankato, MN: The Child's World, 2012.

Montgomery, Anne. *Solid or Liquid?* Huntington Beach, CA: Teacher Created Materials, 2015.

Reilly, Kathleen M. *Explore Solids and Liquids!* White River Junction, VT: Nomad Press, 2014.

On the Web

Visit our Web site for links about ice cream:
childsworld.com/links

Note to Parents, Teachers, and Librarians: We routinely verify our Web links to make sure they are safe and active sites. So encourage your readers to check them out!

Index

About the Author

Meg Gaertner is a children's book author and editor who lives in Minnesota. When not writing, she enjoys dancing and spending time outdoors.